Fantastic Frogs

Written by
Cath Jones

There are about 7,000 different kinds of frogs.

Frogs are good jumpers. They have long, strong legs to help them jump.

This frog is jumping out of the water.

Frogs have big eyes that look as if they are stuck on top of the frog's head.

This helps the frog see all around. Frogs can see ahead, to the side and behind them. This means they can spot a **predator** who might want to eat them.

What do frogs sound like?

They can make lots of different sounds. Sometimes it sounds as if they can croak, bark, moo, bleat, quack and click!

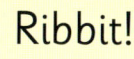
Ribbit!

Where can you find frogs?

Many frogs have their home underwater, but some frogs make their home under the ground or on land.

Frogs have strong legs so they can swim well.

Many kinds of frogs are **nocturnal**. This means that they come out at night to hunt and feed. In the daytime, they hide and sleep.

Sometimes frogs are hard to see. They blend in with their background.

This helps keep them safe. It makes it harder for a predator to see them.

This frog looks like the moss on the tree.

Where do frogs come from?

A frog starts as an egg. Then they grow like this:

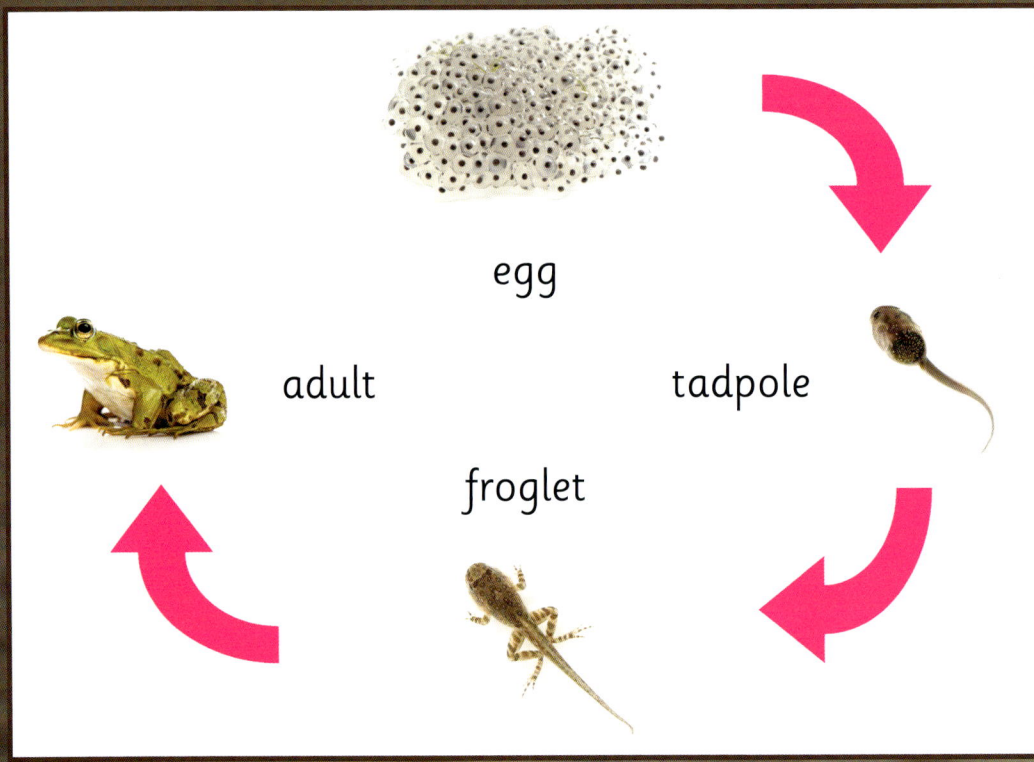

The eggs of frogs clump together.
This is **frog spawn**.

Tadpoles come from the eggs.

At first the tadpoles have no legs, but they do have a tail. As they grow, their tails get shorter and legs start to appear. They start to look like little frogs, or froglets.

Then they turn into frogs.

What do frogs eat?

Frogs are **carnivores**. This means that they eat meat – perhaps insects or snakes!

This frog is grabbing a cricket for its lunch.

Some frogs shed their skin as they grow. Then they eat the old skin. (It is good food for the frogs!)

This frog is shedding its skin and eating it.

Tree frogs

Some kinds of frogs spend all their time in trees. They are called tree frogs.

Tree frogs can jump in the trees well. They have long fingers and toes to grip the twigs and branches of the trees.

Some kinds of tree frog spend all their time in the trees. They never come down to the ground!

Do not eat me!

Many kinds of frogs have a good trick to avoid getting eaten.

They have poison in their skin.

If a predator eats a poison frog, it will get ill and maybe it will die.

The predators soon find out which frogs have poison in them!

Sometimes poison frogs have bright red, yellow or blue skin. This says, "Don't eat me! I can kill you!"

This frog is a **poison dart frog**.

It looks cute, but you must keep clear. It could kill you!

Eating frogs

Some people like to eat frogs' legs. They cook the legs in a pan with garlic, butter and pepper. Sometimes they make frogs' legs soup.

Would you like some?